being you
a journal

ELENA BROWER

sounds true
BOULDER, COLORADO

To Jonah and James

I am.

I FeeL.

I DO.

I Love.

I SPeAK.

I See.

I unDerSTanD.

I TruST.

I ACT.

introduction

"There is a wilderness in every person, a way of walking, a set of spots, a blinking impulse that silently draws us forward." TOKO-PA TURNER

The book you hold in your hands is your chance to tend to your inner wilderness, cultivate an abiding sense of safety, connect to your creativity, and move toward your highest inner consciousness.

Since the age of nine, I've kept diaries and journals; this private conversation nurtures my inner life and continues to be vital to my overall health. Connecting to ourselves, learning to trust ourselves, and actively loving ourselves is crucial if we are to be of service in the world today.

In these pages, take time to quietly observe what's happening inside in order to craft your innermost dialogue and your outward responses. Let this work create the necessary pause when things feel overwrought. Let this journal serve as a refuge in which to honor your experiences and shape your life from the inside out.

May this work invite you to accept and heal what hurts. May your healings become the ways you'll change the world.

May this book bring you true and lasting ease in Being You.

CHOOSING MYSELF
WHAT ATTRIBUTES AM I CHOOSING TO CULTIVATE WITHIN MYSELF?

what am i actively avoiding?

where and with whom am i frozen?

WHERE AND WITH WHOM AM I BEING
TOO CONTROLLING?
(TRYING TO MAKE THINGS HAPPEN THAT
AREN'T MEANT TO BE)

WHERE AND WITH WHOM AM I BEING
TOO PERMISSIVE?
(ALLOWING THINGS TO HAPPEN THAT
SHOULDN'T HAPPEN TO ME)

emotion BECOMES MOOD BECOMES STATE

can i choose my emotions?

THESE are THE EMOTIONS I'M CHOOSING TODAY.

THESE are THE emotions i cHoose To reDuce negativity.

THESE are THE emotions i cHoose To amplify positivity.

tenderness

THIS IS HOW i STRENGTHEN my TENDERNESS.

I am sacred. I am open to receive. I am closed to negativity. I am listening.

Consensuality Exercises

Introduction

Who are you?

Regretful

Do you have any regrets?

Are your regrets due to a lack of action?

Regrets

Actions | Words

Feelings | Thoughts

We shouldn't regret thoughts and feelings, we should only be concerned when thoughts & feelings turn into actions or words that hurt others. I do.

every action or behavior
is a **pattern**
emerging from a
process
that's
been
long in
the making.

what is emerging

TODAY
?

can i trace the
origins of it?

can i see way back to
where that pattern began?

can i begin
a new

pattern,

a new

process?

WHAT DOES THAT

LOOK LIKE?

these are the people who inspire me with their journey.
and these are the things they do, which i can emulate
in my own way.

choosing to address my grief

allows for clear vision.

WHAT AM I GRIEVING?

ACCEPT

in the north.
be real. be vulnerable.
let time pass and
teach you all.

FEEL

in the west.
there might be
more to discover.
be brave.

BEGIN

in the east.
allow the sadness
to unfurl.

SOLIDIFY

in the south.
honor your sadness,
and recognize your
resilience.

contradiction
is a creative force.

contradiction is fertile ground for growth and awakening.

THIS IS THE CONTRADICTION i am managing.

[the lie i was told; the confusion to which i was exposed]

this is what is **changing** or **emerging** today.

boundary: a line that marks the limits of an area

PHYSICAL BOUNDARIES ARE SACRED.

MENTAL BOUNDARIES ARE EQUALLY SACRED.

This is what i allow into my mind.

this is whom i allow into my mind.

altar: a sacred space in which i make offerings of my art and my presence

I am the altar.

THIS IS WHAT I PLACE HERE.

Be
resolution-
oriented.

communicate
my FEELINGS.

honor
myself.

claim
space
TO
heal.

trust my
intuition.

" know and honor which actions are **self-respecting** and which are not. "
                                                    - Pixie Lighthorse

i love.

THIS IS MY DEFINITION OF LOVE.

LOVE

EXAMPLES OF love:

- ALMOST EVERY DAY, i HAVE to FORGIVE MYSELF FOR SOMETHING. THAT'S LOVE.

- TREATING MYSELF THE WAY i WOULD TREAT SOMEONE IMPORTANT to ME.

- ASKING FOR HELP WHEN ASKING ISN'T COMING NATURALLY. THAT'S ALSO LOVE.

my **worthiness** was never stolen...

i inadvertently disowned it.

my capacity for self-love can be dimmed, but never taken from me.

this is why i am worthy of a healthy relationship.

this is why i am worthy of love.

this is why i am worthy of success.

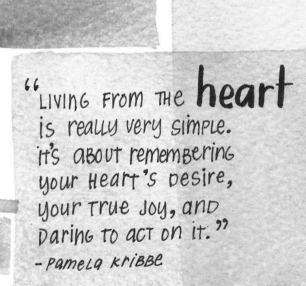

" LIVING FROM THE **heart**
is really very simple.
it's about remembering
your HEART'S Desire,
your TRUE Joy, and
DARing TO ACT ON it. "

- Pamela kribbe

harmony

I am learning to

Love my adversaries,
Those who reveal and
reflect some trace of
negativity within me.
This is a love that
welcomes me to a
new form of freedom
beyond resentment,

toward Harmony,

which is

Grace.

inner dignity

where does it live in me?

Can i amplify it? Is it Love? Is it Different?

THIS IS AN

EXAMPLE

OF HUMILITY THAT

RESONATES WITH ME.

THIS IS WHERE I'M LEARNING

TO BE humble.

humility is a practice of holding myself in perspective. is remembering that i'm part of a much larger whole.

when i am **humble**, i am willing to fearlessly, truthfully ask for help and receive it with elegance.

where does **love** live in humility?

These pages remind me of the *love* that lives in me.

i speak.

i can
" learn to
communicate
my feelings
by sitting
with them
before i
speak.
"

pixie
LIGHTHorse

THESE are THE FEELINGS i NEED TO SiT WITH RiGHT now.

my words have power.

 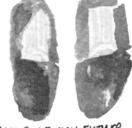

my words are the seeds of my future.

these are the words i choose.

LISTEN WITH GENTLENESS. I AM LEARNING TO

these are the ways i can help others feel heard, held, and respected.

These are the people with whom I need to have a difficult conversation, and the topics we need to address.

May i have your permission to say something i'm afraid to say?

I am LISTENING.

THANK you FOR TELLING Me.

WORDS TO GUIDE a CHALLENGING Conversation:

can you say more about that?

THESE are THE matters about which i need to speak up.

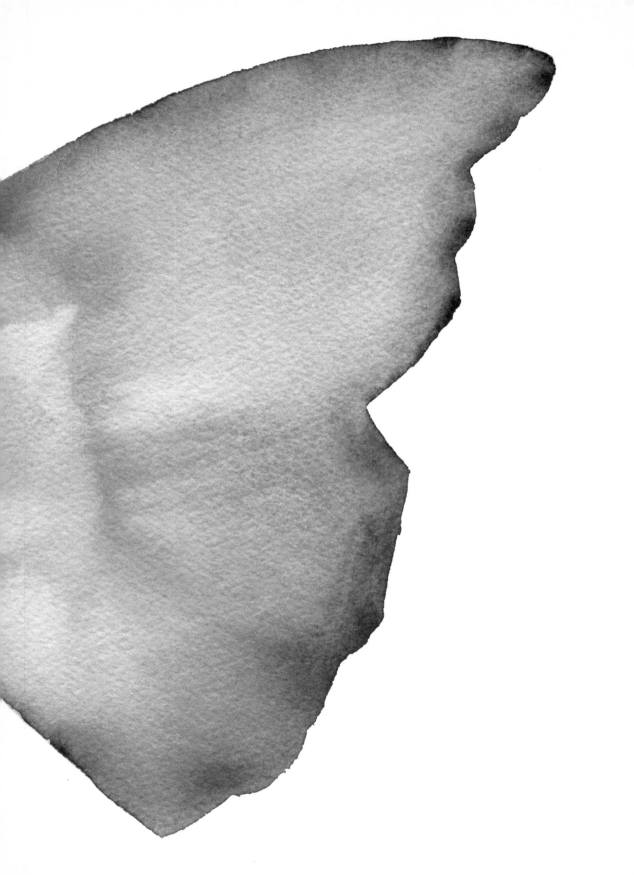

prayer can be any way in which I hold myself. prayer Doesn't need to be spoken. prayer is my innermost broadcast. prayer is my wakeful peacemaking.

may i remain open to learning more when it hurts.

may i open to the wisdom beneath this feeling.

may i remember who i am beneath what needs healing.

may i stay strong in the face of this suffering.

THIS IS WHAT NEEDS TO BE SAID.

THESE are THE BIGGEST QUestions.

i see.

my life is as brilliant as i **envision** it to be.

this is my vision.

THIS IS MY vision.

HOW DO i **see** myself?

THESE are my POSITIVE TRAITS. . . . . . .

THIS IS WHAT I'M LEARNING.

. . . . . THESE are my NEGATIVE TRAITS. . . . .

. . . THANK YOU . . . THANK YOU . . . THANK YOU . . . THANK YOU . . . THANK YOU . . .

THANK YOU FOR HELPING ME SEE EVIDENCE OF

Grace.

my mind is my most
sacred space

these are the THOUGHTS That Bring the most Grace.

THIS is WHERE i see resistance WiTHin MYSELF.

Where I see resistance
I invite evolution.

THERE IS MORE WISDOM BENEATH THE THOUGHTS IN MY MIND.

THIS IS THE WISDOM I CAN SEE TODAY.

THERE is
NOTHING real
ABOUT SEEING
MYSELF as
insignificant
or
insufficient.

WHEN WE FULLY GIVE OUR ATTENTION, WE EXPERIENCE BOTH

POWER and rest.

i understand.

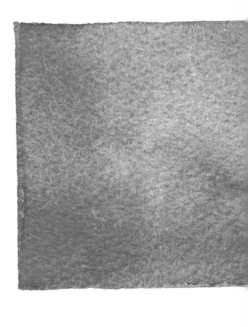

comparison is the thief of

COMPASSION

THESE are   my THOUGHTS

OF compassion

FOR mySELF.

Some part of me knows how to heal this.

THESE are THE attitudes THAT might Be obscuring my understanding.

THESE are THE attitudes THAT Will allow my understanding to evolve.

SOLITUDE:

patiently and silently

returning Home to myself

recipe

FOR

HEALING

i see and stand in the pain. i observe it as energy.

i release any contraction by EXPANDING open.

i release my judgments about the pain.

these are the choices that help me heal.

when i rest in prayer

i let go of masks, patterns, assumptions.

i open to what else is possible.

These are my **prayers** for clear understanding.

increasing my willingness to be

Less certain, more free.

i trust.

every thought i have contributes to love or fear.

THESE are THE HABITS I CULtivate to **Trust myself.**

These are the relations I nurture to consistently experience belief in myself.

It's safe for me to trust and relax into my gifts.

THESE are some of my GIFTS.

we don't have secrets;
secrets have us.
these are the secrets i release in order to trust.

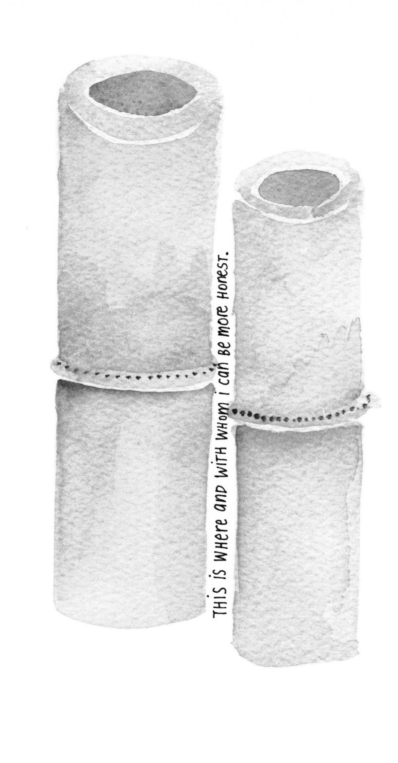

This is where and with whom I can be more honest.

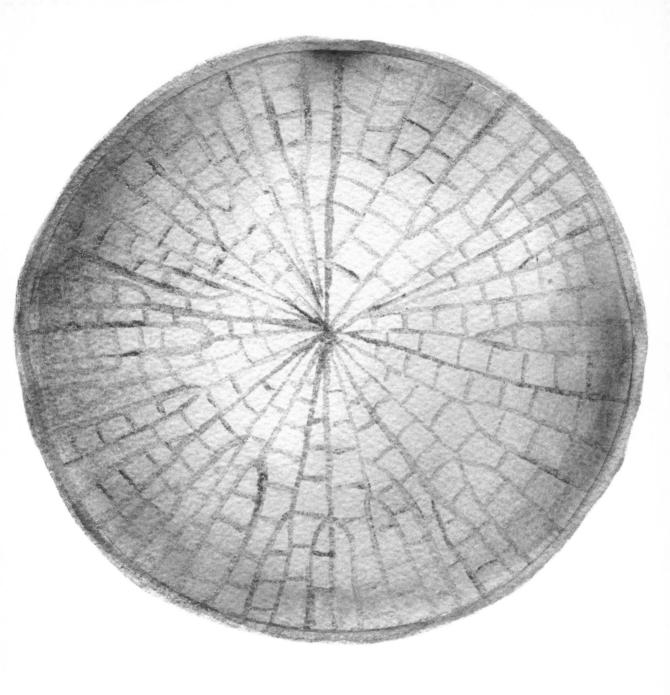

WHO invites you to safely grow and expand?

Thank them here.

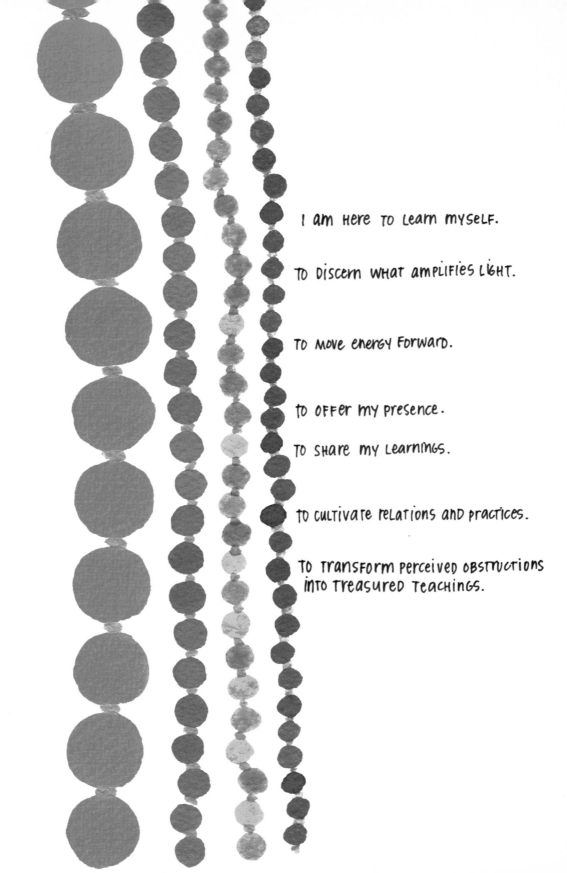

I am here to learn myself.

To discern what amplifies light.

To move energy forward.

To offer my presence.

To share my learnings.

To cultivate relations and practices.

To transform perceived obstructions into treasured teachings.

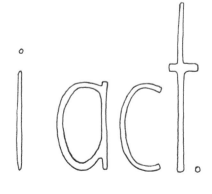

ACTIVISM:

actions I take to shape and contribute to my community and our world.

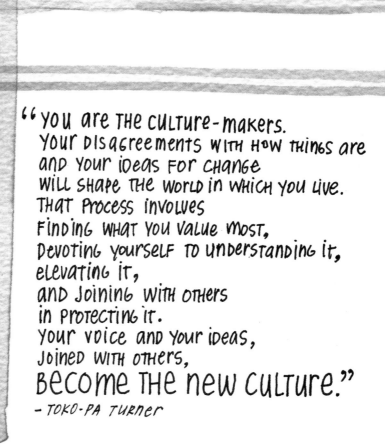

"You are the culture-makers.
Your disagreements with how things are
and your ideas for change
will shape the world in which you live.
That process involves
finding what you value most,
devoting yourself to understanding it,
elevating it,
and joining with others
in protecting it.
Your voice and your ideas,
joined with others,
BECOME THE NEW CULTURE."

— TOKO-PA TURNER

I AM NOT perfect.

I Am Perfect

THESE are the CHANGES THAT need TO HAPPEN IN my world.

THESE
are the ways
in WHICH
I WILL HELP
THOSE
CHANGES
COME ABOUT.

priority

is not a matter of
IMPORTANCE;
it's the way in which
i arrange my experience.

MY PRIORITIES RIGHT NOW:

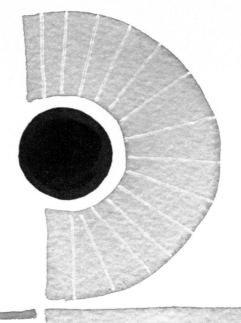

I am strengthened by hardship.

THIS IS HOW
HARDSHIP
makes me
STRONGER.

risk GOES AGAINST MY BRAIN'S DESIRE TO STAY AS IS.

THE LAST TIME I TOOK A risk THAT STRENGTHENED ME, THIS HAPPENED.

THESE ARE THE RISKS I'M CONSIDERING IN THE FUTURE.

THIS IS WHAT'S HOLDING ME BACK FROM TAKING THOSE RISKS RIGHT NOW.

THIS IS HOW IT WILL FEEL

TO overcome those Limits.

Success is not about what I know. Success is the cumulative effect of what I do.

THESE are THE
ACTIONS
I take toward the
HEALING
OF THE WORLD.

reflections

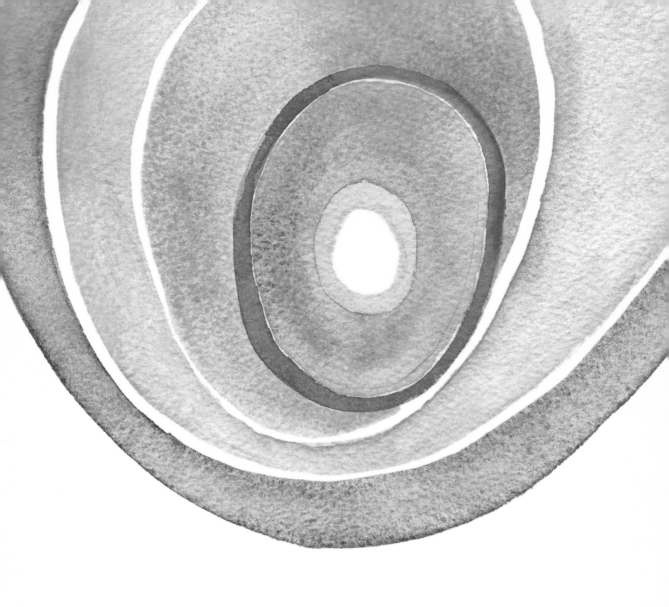

Acknowledgments

Thank you, Jonah, for inspiring me to be a better human.

Thank you, Mama, for always staying near and sending all the signs.

Thank you, James Benard, for your heart and soul as I work and live as your lucky and thankful partner.

Thank you, Kevin Sullivan, of Benard Creative. Your work and input on this book is invaluable and enduring. And thank you, Abbi Newfeld, for your valued hours of careful scanning and organizing.

Thank you, Jenny Murray, for every hour and ounce of your energy, love, dedication, and commitment.

Thank you, my family—Daddy, Sue, Jessie, Jeff, Cory, Lou, and Marie—for always supporting and believing.

Thank you, Sounds True, for your faith and trust in my work.

Thank you, Lynn Hazan, for all you do to make my life easeful.

Thank you, King Art, for the copious art supplies—a true gift.

Thank you, Lisa Brooks, for introducing me to Wildthorne watercolors. And thank you, Kim Wildthorne, for crafting the most sumptuous, enriching paints for my work.

Thank you, Queen Michelle Martello and King Zane Gibbs, for being my favorite catalysts.

Thank you, Toko-pa Turner, Pixie Lighthorse, Tanya Markul, Ruth King, and Maya Angelou for your commitment. Your work has elevated everything for me.

Thank you, Roshi Joan Halifax, for quietly guiding my way with your grace in these formative times.

Thank you, Handel Group. Traces of your magic are all over this work.

Thank you, Ally Bogard and Chloe Crespi, for being the best friends a girl could dream up.

Thank you, dear soul family, for offering up your dining room tables so I could finish these pages: Michael Rothman, Scooter and Libby Weintraub, Lysa Cooper, Dr. Douglas Brooks and Susan Pullman-Brooks. I love each of you more than words can say.

about the author

Elena Brower is a mama, author, teacher, and artist. Devoted to the healing practices of meditation, yoga, and contemplative writing, her journal *Practice You* is beloved worldwide. Her first book, *Art of Attention*, has now been translated into six languages, and her online coursework is highly regarded for bringing analog creativity to virtual spaces. She's developed two audio programs with Sounds True, *The Return Home* and *Grounded and Free*. Listen to her renowned *Practice You* podcast at practiceyou.com, and experience yoga and meditation with Elena at glo.com.

about Sounds True

Sounds True is a multimedia publisher whose mission is to inspire and support personal transformation and spiritual awakening. Founded in 1985 and located in Boulder, Colorado, we work with many of the leading spiritual teachers, thinkers, healers, and visionary artists of our time. We strive with every title to preserve the essential "living wisdom" of the author or artist. It is our goal to create products that not only provide information to a reader or listener but also embody the quality of a wisdom transmission.

For those seeking genuine transformation, Sounds True is your trusted partner. At SoundsTrue.com you will find a wealth of free resources to support your journey, including exclusive weekly audio interviews, free downloads, interactive learning tools, and other special savings on all our titles.

To learn more, please visit SoundsTrue.com/freegifts or call us toll-free at 800.333.9185.

Sounds True
Boulder, CO 80306

© 2021 Elena Brower

Sounds True is a trademark of Sounds True, Inc.

All rights reserved. No part of this book may be used or reproduced in any manner without written permission from the author(s) and publisher.

Published 2021

Cover design by Rachael Murray

Book design by Meredith March

Cover image and interior art © Elena Brower

Printed in South Korea

ISBN 978-1-68364-712-6

10 9 8 7 6 5 4 3 2 1